Ojo de la Cueva

Ojo de la Cueva

Cordelia Candelaria

 maize press • mazorca series

maize press
the colorado college
colorado springs, co. 80903

Acknowledgments

"Cliffs," was published under the title "Thoughts of My Desert Home V" in *RiverSedge,* 1982. The following poems were printed in *Grito Del Sol,* 1976: "Crated," which originally appeared under the title "Coachella Valley, 1973"; "Within," appeared under the title "Thoughts of My Desert Home I"; "Baby Rocks, Arizona," appeared under the title "Thoughts of My Desert Home VII"; and "Windstorm at the Gallup Intertribal Fair," appeared under the title "Thoughts of My Desert Home VIII." "The Fall," and "In the Bengal Lair, A Poet" were originally printed in the *Rocky Mountain Review.* "Teenage Son," originally titled "Celebrations of a Spring Peeper VII," and "Heading North," originally titled "Past Wolf Creek Pass to the Teton Range," were first printed in *Rendezvous.* "Segments" originally appeared in the *Rocky Mountain Review of Language and Literature.*

ISBN: 0-939558-08-4
Library of Congress Catalog Number: 84-060897

Printed in the United States of Ameria.

This project is supported by a grant from the National Endowment for the Arts in Washington, D.C., a Federal agency and The Colorado College in Colorado Springs, Colorado.

Contents

*To my brother Edward Chávez (1938-1975) because
he inspired me in childhood, to my husband Fidel
because he inspires me today, and to our son Clifford
because he's my inspiration for the future, I dedicate
these poems con mucho cariño y agradecimiento.*

In Line

I thought this lifetime
i could write a poem.

To my surprise
while at the check-out counter
clerk went seeking change

and i just wait.

Graffiti Semiotics

leaving the library
    eye weary
        soul wringered

into parchment
    she revolved herself
        out of the walls

of truth and met
    a scrawl

Pussy

how specific
    the thing
        the need
how hypnotizing

two steps away
    etched loud and clear

Cock

for all the world to see
    to wince
        to know
the origin of signs

Ojo de la Cueva

Out here in Ojo de la Cueva
the New Year's snowstorm has left
our desert artificial – bereft
of its unyielding dirt brown, now covered

by snow sifted dryly on the rocks.
The white on sagebrush seems soldered
enamel, not frozen rain watered
by an ancient *mata* atop Midnight Mesa.

In the distance the pumphouse
startles with its silhouettes of jade
on the wall, spidery lines espaliered
by a tricky sun's sculpting glare

splintered through the *chamizal.*
Here in this hot dryscape our resisting
iced white stems from long habit, from encysting
nodules growing inside our cactus roots.

———————

Midnight Mesa lies north of the arroyo in Ojo de la Cueva, New Mexico.

11

A Dios

domingo	Nothing more beautiful
	than a peach-tinted desert sky
	at sunrise, O Dios,
lunes	How dated You are, You're
	not upper case today
	you're a dios
martes	Lowered to impotence
	beneath an alphabet
	of A-bombs H-bombs
miércoles	The alpha and omega
	of megabomb
	sunsets, hay dios,
jueves	Nothing uglier
	than a grease-fried egg forgotten
	on a plate, cold and revolting
viernes	In its yellow-yolked hardness
	meal to a busy fly
	settled on its shiny scum,
saba Dios	O Dios, la noche llega
	sin luna, sin luz
	sin día adiós.

Crated

a Proustian memory du temps perdu

Crated clusters of grapes
beckoned by the long black finger
del patron, el freeway,
lined with picket-waving bodies
repeating el grito – que viva!
once more.

Y siempre la bandera:
blazoning red, jagged black, scarce
white in windblown waves reminding
of past cabrito picnics near narrow ríos

where mama washed clean the goatheads,
sending bloodripples over craggy rocks,
coal dark beneath flowing cloud wisp
reflections. Cabezitas roasting,

we spun flat stones hard across that river,
today's asphalt trimmed suburbia
where brand new el dorados wait without.

Cliffs

cliffs of red earth
skirted round
by flat brown dirt
   generations
   of unmoving rugged red
   on merest brown
   flattening
   where the horizon
   billow-capes blue
Kayenta, Arizona,
my folks live there
in a trailer
hear gaping Black Mesa
   sangre y lágrimas
   de carbón
   modern-day Toxcatl

(Black Mesa is the site of one of the world's largest strip-mining operations by the Peabody Coat Company. During the Conquest the Spaniards destroyed the Aztecs' Main Temple in a bloody massacre during the fiesta de Toxcatl.)

Within

Within a Midwest water bubble
dripping and sliming inside
some new moist self,
I think of dry
of drought sun showers and charred sand
stretching beyond the farthest point
where Shiprock warns the humid sodden:
beware of pregnant deserts.

I think but cannot feel or taste
cactus touches
prickling me awake.

That far-off fresh aridity
pure exact meticulously alive
beckons the itching barefoot squirming
inside my damp dull heart —
so like the unwonted sludge without.

Baby Rocks, Arizona

Touch this sand i sift for you
from boulder's shaded side: damp.
Compare this handful
from open sun's share
facing west toward red cliff
B a b y   R o c k s.
Warm warm sand; infant's brow
in fever, beat fast fast heart beat
you even hear between baby's sighs.

    O, mountain of soft rocks
    red boulders and pebbles rippling
    upon hot flatland   who
    christened you?   What
distant Apache mata sought then
to stone me stone me   O!
Little Son's dead

(Baby Rocks stands on the northeast corner of Arizona.)

Windstorm at the Gallup Intertribal Fair

twisting above mesa's distant levels
like so much cotton candy
or so little
whirl of sand

funnels over horizon's arc
blowing a stretch of universe
large as my fingernail
bitten off in haste and sweet

and merry-goes-round and ferris wheels
and directionless navajo falling feet
design new sand paintings –
leaving the storm ahead.

Haciendo Tamales

Haciendo tamales mi mamá wouldn't compromise —
no mftr chili, no u.s.d.a. carne
nomas handgrown y home-raised, todo.
Oregano had to be wildly grown
in brown earth bajo la sombra.
Tamale wrappers had to be hojas
dried from last year's corn
nurtured by sweat — ¿como no?
Trabajos de amor pa'enriquecer el saborcito.
To change or country
she wouldn't sacrifice her heritage.
Entonces, como su mamá antes y su abuelita
she made her tamales from memory
cada sabor nuevo
como el calor del Westinghouse where
she cooked them with gas under G.E. lights —
bien original to the max!

You

You lasted between my legs beyond the night.
Today your weight and movement yet strain
The muscles of each inner thigh, still press
Against my private nerves. But this soreness
Only hints at the tantalizing secrets
Playing out their quiet thrill inside,
Warming to an urgent pleasant ache
Where last I warmed you. And these secrets
Only echo something else within me still —
The substance — or matter — or realness
Of your caring every minute of one night.
Like love it lingers to compel a smile
Now and then and will long outlive the pain.

Segments

She peeled the orange tenderly
as if it were a letter from a lover.
Air became tangy citrus mist
caressing every fragrant breath she took.

She pulled the fruity wedge
from its vulnerable whole and sucked
it soft. Fingers of oily sweetness
clung to all she touched, orange prints

separate from the tender hand placing
peel and seed and stringy membrane
into another mass of parts.
Sweet grip on a segment of her life.

Come

Come warm my bed.
Come fill this waiting space
lying empty, like a late spring
garden plot needing to be tilled.
Place yourself right close to me –
aquí – so I can breathe
your wondrous strength within me
deep, the most missed smell of you
and just as the juniper
beside la noria at Camp wraps itself
around that desert rock there,
allá en Gobernador,
you will return my touch, my love.

Warm my bed. Come

Smeared

smeared teardrops
wet cheeks
the sky's colors
blur into each other

the faded ocher sunset
can't hide the chill riding the evening
like dampness sneaking 'longside
a morning sun

"How much longer till nightfall?"

the car's motor sounds the silence
spaced between them
driver   and   passenger
traveling long distances
apart

Where?

Where, then, those early carousel days
Of ride and upndown and round,
Of tinkling music deep inside, of
Pearly slips down the Milky Way?

      Where's the magic reveille?
Bundles of bundles we stumble, looped tight
Like i u d coils spun ready to spring
We rummage inside ourselves.

Out, then, out of that warm cliché:
We're spinning our wheels, man, spin
Ning. Time to move to the distant hum
Of that carnival we shared in the rain.

Ashes

We were one
Like the old tree stump
In the distant corner of our land
Wildflowers shooting out its sunken core
Clinging along its crusty bark

Then we needed firewood
And you took your axe and cleanly split
Cleanly split into two halves
    The trunk
You didn't stop you hacked each half
In half and cleanly split the little halves
Chipping splinters far away
From that once big, sapless trunk.
    What fires it made!
Crackling crisply carelessly
Lighting up former shadows in the room
Exposing the gaping corner

The Fall

In that prehistory
When time meant only
Sunwarmth/starlight love —
Before consequences
Weighted every tenderness to earth,
Mudlike,
Your flaws compelled,
Like primal signs,
Cave paintings etched within me
To show from whence you came,
How far with me you traveled
Toward the light

Of a crisp clear day
And your wife,
Grocery sacks burdening her walk,
Forced record-keeping on us.

Minutes roll round to duties.
Your smile bothers me
Your hand upon my shoulder
Lies heavy in me.

Homely Burden

Longing is an agony of homely burden
the heart's dishwashing, private
unworthy of any show
not to be shared or
lingered over
or retold as truer fact
in fussy phrases from a poet's store.
Plain gut – longing
(from innermost rib and tenderest lining
of an urgent cavity)
defies conceit.
That raw pleasure of discomfort
presses muscle and mind toward center
tightly
steady
no abstractions
just press in
private and sure.

This agony of the ordinary
began with sculptor's struggle with his welder
(brilliant sun-tipped torch that once
killed even vision with its sparkler glow
of metal – they say it blinds you if you watch)
when mainline broke
torch shrunk to apology
averted eyes
dull longing.

I Can See

"I can see clearly now
    the rain must fall"
Sunset frosted clouds
    venom lacquered love
        breeze   like red-rimmed shrubs.
        by
Shimmer lacèd stars
    murky mildewed glances
        coil in   staccato stares.
        into
Lightning breaking skies
    tender febrile phrases
        echo round   ambivalent us.
        about
    Welling soft beyond the edge
    sorrow swells –
Teardrops plashing on a subdued smile.

With Edward and Tesa

For Clifford

In the 7th grade you investigated
insects, frogs, and rodents, and
introduced your desert family
to Spring Peeper's charms
especially the sexual ones.
A delightful frog we learned
that peeps and breeds all spring long
to the thrilling joy of you then,
a pimpling son investigating swamps.

You taught us to appreciate
Spring Peeper's natural subtlety
while hiding marshy colored
in marches. I thought their dorsal mark
(a cross +) a sign of blessedness —
you, the iconoclast, laughed.
Morning's alarm that spring
sprang from the depths of your echo
ing throat shrill but sure.

So to wake you now
these verses —
      s
     p
      r
       i
        n
         g
         !

You Looked Up

Then you looked up
Overwhelmingly wide
Eyed, gazed directly
Into my eyes and nodded
Wisely before returning
To the suck.

That instant I found
This love
And breath was newer
Than the first glimpse
Of Red Mountain Peak rising
In the Ouray Range horizon

Lost at Tadpole Creek

That day you and your buddy
Explored the distances
Behind your houses,
Along the ugly alley to 'Dolfito's
Harness shop and found,
As you were lost,
The trashy barely flowing creek
Of tadpoles wiggling to your fancy —
I was sore troubled.

All that hour we looked
And looked for you,
Your silly pretend lances
Spied near Mama Carmel's woodpile,
Your muddied face of sheer surprise
At seeing *me* so far from home
("Back there" where I belonged) —
I found the rest of you.

Teenage Son

Staring at a slip of winter sunrise

At a cool red ball reluctantly ascending
I am stopped by the moment,

      the world's teetering balance
      between heavy pendant gray
      and fuzzy swelling peach

A blink of eyelids
I'm still staring
But I've missed the movement:
The darkness vacuumed into orange daybirth
Day sounds   day creatures   daylife filling.

      when did you become a frog?

Fall Colors

Autumn nestles in the yard
inside a gold and scarlet mask
awaiting the early dark calmly.

Should I thus settle into my fate
away from you, shed all feeling
and quietly outlast the missing?

Can't.
My leaves fall in hard splashes
and soak my mask to winter shreds.

To Manhood

Back of the house below the hill
the Animas hides its power this March
before the spring run-off starts in earnest
and snowcaps from the highest Rockies
become bold currents in mid-June.

We try and try to know how high the flow
will flow, how fast its foam will speed.
We wonder if the piñon jetty will break away
at last, pine cones crashing in the current
                        you come to mind.

Swirling among those thoughts
one turns to what you'll be the coming years
to where you'll find the perfect
image of yourself to hold up
to the one you leave behind with us.

My throat numbs to feel the pain
you'll feel in love, my faith
still in its joy. And over the river
a clear sun melts into tomorrow —
glazing the edges shiny and hot on my cheeks.

---

*El Río de las Ánimas Perdidas, or "the Animas", crosses Durango,
Colorado.*

"Don't Call Me So Much, Ma,
Now That I'm Staying With Gina"

Fight to keep from calling
right hand prevents left
and writes a poem
instead of punching seven digits
to your life
newer than it was at seven pounds
of shiny flesh
when i could hold you
call you without thought.
   Don't really wonder
   about her
   about you together
   i wonder what to do
   with all that mothered you
   all that inside me
   around me
   like im carrying something
   i should unload somewhere
   like i forgot to tell something
   on the tip of my tongue
   that blew gum bubbles for you
   i wonder if it all will shrink
   to workable size
   if that's how mothers get wrinkles
   wearing the extra large pattern
   of love
   that once fit smooth but now
   just folds and creases in surprise.

Traces

Slipping into tangled flannel
Bumping into sunrise dim kitchen
To make coffee, finally I see
    The filled ashtray
    Jutting out at table's edge.
Up late the night before
Reading and smoking till dawn
And sleep overtook him
(Feet cold in bed).

Carelessly
I push the ashtray to safety
Hurry to awaken school-kids
And trip on lopsided basketball
Left bounceless beside a fallen airpump.
    Surrounded by the purity
    Of sleeping children helplessly entranced
    By dreams and vague departing dark
    (Basketball scuffle echoes),

Deliberately
I aim the ball to corner's clutter
Up! Up!
    (hints of night
    disappear come light
    but afterward
    in inner places
    there're always traces.)

Fish Heads

The night was warm for family gatherings
Spring-crisp air awakening the winter's dead.
Custom says we start anew
Do fresh things to shake away December's ash

      like overturn a long forgotten plank
      to uncover the startling motion
      of insect towns or see a clear night's
      Milky Way that proves the crowdedness
      of empty space or hear the flutter din
      of ducks heading north again.

The family littles spun natural child whirls
Little suns forming distant galaxies of light.
The middle two exiting youth's orbit
Moved toward our own like comets from afar.
And on this planet earth the family gathered
With many fine connecting lines of love
Fear pain and laughter neatly intersecting
Opposites as well. Into that pulsing universe
May 23rd, our neighbor crashlanded,
Bringing the lower realm of family
A trout heads treat, water fresh, bleeding still—

      and in that lively world of worlds,
      a month exact before a brother dies,
      that act—drunk Joe's fish heads
      for the cats—pulled gravity home again.

Pretend

*on the way home from
my brother's funeral*

pretend i'm a tree sister said
a tree tucked in the corner of a nursery
    comes along
    on a day unseasonably cold
    wet earth on his shoes, the gardener
    black peat on his trousers
    still sleepy or tired,
    not whistling his usual
    a u t u m n   l e a v e s
    and even in fullness my branches quiver
    awaiting anew old summer's late warmth

    He aims at my tree heart
    And pierces and prunes
    Forgetting it seems
    I've already been cut.
    Then as the sap flows
    Deep within I hurt a loss
    Hurt a loss in me,
    Not a branch lost, not a twig
    Nor a leaf but the end of a core
    Of a core of me

Heading North

for a dead brother

Heading north this evening
on a road you traveled too
two huge and tufty clouds collided
        – WHAP! –
they crashed and blocked
the setting sun from view.
For an instant, maybe three,
the sun and clouds struck
an explosion of light and dark,
a harmony of jarring chords in air
        – O Singing One –
that shifted soon into your painting
of webbed contrasts, "memory."
        Again I thought
if only he could see.

Did You Die

Did you die before
or after we moved to Durango? I forget
if we talked about the beauty of the river's name
"Río de las animas pérdidas"? Did we share
a hearing of "Send in the Clowns" or
was that only in my dreams of you in June?
I think we walked by the yucca on Midnight Mesa
one spring but then I remember
we didn't live here seven years ago. I think
we argued about whose "Borrachita" is better
Miguél's or Trío de los Panchos, but then
I'm reminded you were
someone else. Did we really talk
about "El Topo" and "Apocalypse Now" or
was that just my wondering what
you'd say and how
you'd sing "those little town blues"
and how you'd paint the children's fort
across the arroyo and how
you'd see the weathered cedar
casting jagged shadows by the new house
and how the Halloweens still sing
your birthday even in this rain.

Beyond Grief: Nuclear Frieze

When in the course of events too human
to give us hope in words however noble
            in cures of mortals born,
the loss of sense consumes us beyond grief—

—and there's the obscene rub.

We cannot weep in simple witness of our grief—
                our loss—
while others ignoring history's threat
preach in jubilation over nuclear might
ignore the threat of history.

Not to be seems no answer to the poet's question.
We cannot honor honor in our time.

A child caught in a windstorm home from school
trembles in fear. Leaves and trash collect
against a chain-link fence. Winds blow
the chaos east then north
        west then south
                commanding coats and scarves
and bodies flailing to stay on course in the wind.
The child lands against the fence
        fingers curl tightly around three links each hand
        face presses against the grate
        eyes see only fragments in random contact
                in the whirl.

An atom trapped inside our global cell.

Criminals

Newspaper's merciless in reminding us
they share the planet with our averageness.
They frighten and fascinate
and terror hypnotizes
forces us to keep them in front
of our eyes assaulting
        tearing her lingerie
           to newsprint shreds
        shooting his left ventricle
        precisely.
You wonder what they do. How
they live their lives: up early? late?
        Flowered sheets, jam on toast?
When it rains, like tonight, heavy
and cold, do they sit cozy somewhere
reading poems, writing them, plotting
how to kill you
        couplets of murder
        cups of rum
in front of a snug fire, warming toes
making small talk, marking time?

Friend's In Jail

                    but then again
              she's always sort of been
        barred from certain realities

                    by her way
              of heeding sunset's purple
        when we see only red, by her way

                    of stopping
              for the thumbing traveller
        because his rags say Joseph's Coat to her

        but still
                    she did commit a crime
                                of cannabis

        and society's now safe from her
                    for twelve months safe from her
                                society shares

        three kids with her
                    in foster care now
                                but safe from her

        society sleeps sweeter now
                    safer now
                                how?

Herself Portrait

"...*Beauty is momentary in the mind*..."
Wallace Stevens
"Peter Quince at the Clavier"

The light is crucial:
Its hue the weight of dusk
Spliced lightly by occasional shards
From a retreating sun.

The waters should be still
As a watercolor, the plash
Against her flesh a liquid breath
Varnishing her curves to instant shine.

The vague reticence of each move —
Fingertips settling stray locks
Into a ravelled knot of hair — could recall
An untried, patient longing.

And surely each indifferent glance she offers
To the outer reaches of the woody bath
Returns to her another's bawdy gaze.
Sweet favors as she bathes.

An Ancient Alphabet

Out of the shadow of Midnight Mesa three horses come
    tramping toward me
And my belly tightens in my heart like that time the eels
In *Tin Drum* slimed out of the horse's head
Red as raw liver noodles and filled me with hard tickles
Of dread to wake me up before I really heard them
Fighting, knowing my brothers and sisters heard too
In the dark, seeing each other better than in daylight
Feeling the WHUCK of his fist on her flesh, tasting
The salt-sweet horror running down her face motionless
As we, darkknowing, in a past far away as a dead

Language, an ancient alphabet deep-buried beneath strata
And strata of birthdays/deathdays straw dust in time
Suddenly ECHOing clear as cries from La Llorona
They tramp this way, equine and fearsome, real
As the lurking frost in April earth.

Go 'Way from My Window, La Llorona (I)

Get lost, lady! ¡Andale!
Far away and forever! ¡Vete! but not
Like sinks of dirty water swallowed by the drain
To rise again in cesspools, not like
A fat black cucaracha swept away
Returns with crowds at midnight. But vanish,
¡Brujamala! out of my life
Como el sudor de mi sobaco.
You've hounded me beyond belief, scaring
My childhood away from me, spooking
My sleep to reels and reels of horror shows
Until the time
Of my passage afuera de la casa
And the reality of your unreality
Turned me into the taste of moldy brine
At the bottom of a jar, into Goneril
Seeing her father as all fathers with
all mothers.
Married forever in sickness and in sickness
Till death parts them in sickness
And in loudness
At midnight, in beatings and blood
And endings of kisses happily forever
Sickness. Go!
Follow your babies llorando
Into the roiling water del Río de las Ánimas Pérdidas.
Let them stare you clear-eyed into Hell.

On Your Mark, Set, Go!

Every night we get ready for death.
Turn back the covers to a neat triangle
Of fresh laundered topsheet
Scribbled with the pattern of pasts
Cluttered noisy yellow or brown
Colored delirium joy or fright,
And shrewd in setting us up to be
Just this way: as we were but tired.
Pasts as earnest as los campesinos
Tracking along the western shore
Certain as la pizca de uvas
El ritmo de ondas, wave-scrubbed
Memories. Custom's set to serve
Regret — but that's the thorn
For rejecters of ritual
Here it comes ready or not
Seek and find
And tag
You're
IT!

This Winter

This winter I understand white –
The power of color's absence –
The weight of pale heavens falling
And fallen upon everything eyes can see
Or fingertips touch in timid hush.
Do I wish for a green birdsong?
The crimson scent of a rose?
The sweetsoft yellow of an April noon?
    high as a man is tall the snow
    shines in my eyes without break
    rainbow prisms hang
    dagger sharp from frosted eaves
    overlooking a shivering Animas River
    edged in white

Desert Blues

the desert sameness sweeps over us
a duststorm blinding our eyes in teary sand
browning to triteness sky's turquoise
                    or
maybe it's depression
persistent and scary and uglier
than Lady Day's lullabyes of proof

you see a yucca rising
out of impotent rocks
grayer than green struggling
to bloom its huge ivory blossoms
in the sun   joyous
as a sundeck of cancer ward patients

Bound Morpheme

I fear the unsuccess of me
as snowdrifts dread the swift approaching spring
certainties as well postponed as lived
as well ignored as seen.
Its hour will create itself and, generous,
extend a moment to my quivering pronoun
minimal pair of I who unsucceeds as noun
instead of screams to live, to be.

Collision

sometimes i take a cup
and hold it in my hand
and worry that it will unclasp itself
and fall S M A S H to the floor
in jagged pieces of glazed paint
and puzzle – like shards.
i rush to set the cup safely
upon a solid surface
and then the mass begins to quiver
from within itself to shake away
the responsibility on cue
i pat the walnut cabinet
to soothe a shivering child and
certain that all witnesses sleep
i slam the fragile vessel
against the murderous wall

Interruption

He understands me
Like that cow near the barbed wire fence
Understands the speckled bass dripping from his hook
To end this poem interruption later –
Cow eating from the hay bale once cubed
By two careful wires twisted thricely at both ends
Now pulled apart buffalo grass and alfalfa
Strands of straw unravelled from his wife's hair
Upswept over the bucket of red-spumed lakewater
Where other sidefloating fish forget to swim.
Never knowing I already saw
He points to show the cow grazing round
The post, missing the barbs spaced eternally along
My hair tufted loose, half-eaten. He gives me
The fish applauding in his red-splattered hands.
I drop it in the bucket to clap at its own forgetting.

Penis Envy

*On hearing women described
by a host of manly poets*

Do they know me
      To the hairy armpits?
      To my depths of wisdom?
      The plain and complex me?
Like a clever man-dropped formula
Trying to express
The sun's dance with a planet
Or that love tug they call
Gravity – a dazzling bit of cleverness –
What they know me to be reflects
The inner membranes of their warty
Wits – that looking glass of slime
Showing Narcissus unto himself
That place where curving thigh
Descends from rounded heaving breasts
And leads inevitably, interesting as
A guided tour – leads
To a center of wet warmth.
      Lover. Mother. Muse.
Weak ejaculations of a masturbating mind.

Pair of Ragged Claws

We can't go there, you and I,
for that evening isn't suited
to this newly shrunken sky.

No more roses on time's rood,
paltry men on sticks, no longer
tastes of liquors never brewed.

Now we tell it as it is
and today is rootless born,
full-blown *deus ex machina,* this:
                sagging skies
                    like
                    washed-out
                    levis
                droop over faceless
                bodies clashing by day
                making alibis
                by night

To WC Williams

Nothing depends
on her plump leg sheathed
in a sheer gray stocking crossed over
her other leg.
Foot tapping on a bare wooden floor.

+

Everything hinges on the chairs
in an empty classroom
looking
like a lunchline
of eager children.

In the Bengal Lair, A Poet

And the Word was made flesh and dwelt among us . . .

Tonight I heard a man
Put forth his actual psyche —
Cleaned up a bit, neatly brushed,
Only the tiniest ooze of blood
And touch of pus
Asserted themselves around the edges,
Otherwise it was a nicely delivered psyche,
Scarcely showing any sign
Of the jagged pain that wrenched it
From its accustomed place
Tucked within a corner of a worn
Battered soul
Shielded by the weathered folds
Of a silver-framed face.

And tonight he did that for us.
Put it there.
Set it out for all the world to see.
And all he gave to ease our task
Of handling another's fresh-scrubbed
Bleeeeding psyche
Was the barest shrug.

The Bengal Lair at Idaho State University is the site of numerous readings.

Ojo de Dios

Not an ordinary eye, staring
Coldly fixed or glazed
Or trembling like a tiny gob of jelly,
Nor peacock hued. Not this eye.
      It is merely perfect.
Peering out each strung layer
Of dyed wool, sheared, river-washed,
Carded and discarded, dyed to colorful
Deaths, intricate eyebeams weave
Angles and arcs that crisscross
Strangely to our depths, or, empty,
Probe and peel right through.
Two simple sticks, four certain corners,
One focused eye.
Were it less than yarn
      It would be godly. Nomas, No mas.

An Ojo de Dios or "God's eye" is an artifact of the Southwest.

Lemming

Until today
I thought you were love's lemming,
Past fond creature ever dimming
Dimming in mind's rest.
      And then today
Amidst the jostling subway crowd
I saw
You move toward me
          And
          Startled into motion
My recent tranquility
      Plunged quickly
Headlong into spinning
      Spinning seas.

Days Drift

Days drift slide unnoticed
into one another
hours just long indifferent
this minute that one
just as yesterday
her hair was of one darkness.

Should be more memorable than this
shouldn't it how could it
could it

Warts and Straw

What is it?
          Inside?

Of incipient pain
I feel the scraping, the scratch
before the ooze of blood,
the eyelids' warmth
before the tears
                    drop.

Can it be—?
My winter's here?

          In his eyes
no smiling recognition,
no piercing gleams
that gladden every pore
that now but see my warts.

Now I know how grass aches
when its green evaporates
to parched thirst and straw
and he tingles at another's touch
another's summer
                    summer touch.

No! — In Thunder

Pulling down the snow-covered roof this winter
icicles, glassy and thick, hang longer
each sunset after a day of Rocky Mountain sun.
All sparkles white and shiny and bright   but
       everything melts away
       cold and sharp
       icicles fall,
       wounding
       the earth at last   a child
       learning to talk smiles   shines
       her warm light   but evening comes
       and all hangs   lower
       glassy   cold   heavy

The Falcon Wife

And he learned of finalities
Besides the grave. – Frost's "The Hill Wife"

Bound by the feathers flapping 'round me
I'm free to fly at will.
His will. Be done. To circle
e f f o r t l e s s l y
For him as I was trained.

Perched on his elbow
Dawn's sudden staleness awakens
Another life, before
The maiden flight.

          O!
          Am I a haggard being
          Forced from fancy flight?

Swooping falcon, disobey
Dip down, tear his balls
Deliver them
b l e e e d i n g
Into his ready grave.

          Wing toward open sky
In the ether of your dreams.

In falconry "haggard" refers to a specific type of bird.

61

Faith

Don't think of love
When you're in love
It's not for thought

Don't seek for gold
When rainbows curve
They're not for wealth

Don't hide the cloud
By linings merely silver
Rain leaves water marks

When babies reach
For dusty flecks of air
Believe the world's well.

Director of the Chicano Studies Program at the University of Colorado at Boulder, Cordelia Candelaria also holds an assistant professorship in the English Department. She has published literary criticism, research on Chicanas, and poetry in numerous journals, as well as in encyclopedias, monographs, and anthologies. She has just completed *Chicano Poetry, A Critical Introduction* for Greenwood Press. Her doctorate in American literature and structural linguistics is from the University of Notre Dame. She describes herself as "una hija, hermana, esposa, madre, tia, profesora, y en veces pendeja pero al fin y al cabo soy 'manita de Nuevo Méjico." She commutes between Boulder and her home in Ojo de la Cueva, New Mexico.